A Stroke of Hope

Malthouse African Poetry

By the same Author

A Stroke of Hope

Tayo Olafioye

MALTHOUSE PRESS LTD

Malthouse Press Limited
8, Amore Street, Off Toyin Street, Ikeja,
P.O. Box 500, Ikeja, Lagos State, Nigeria.

Lagos, Benin, Ibadan, Jos, Oxford, Port-Harcourt, Zaria

© Tayo Olafioye 2000
First published 2000
ISBN 978 023

Dedication

To my Eighty Year Old Mother

Elizabeth Olafioye

For her joys and pains of motherhood
over the years.

Gratitude

To my students of the past and present, at home or abroad, I am profoundly thankful to have met you. One generation replaces the other. It never grows old. You have brought me oceans of enrichment and honey beyond your years. If circumstance makes it difficult for me to ever see you again, along the way, please understand and remember me, but do not be sorry. Life evokes its own justice and its inevitable conclusions. I have had a jolly good ride. If I survive, we'll live to smile again.

To my friends, who at various stages have contributed to my scholarship, an immense appreciation from my heart. Heaven's Gold Medal of Paradise to Kim Dettrey, Jason Josafat, Lalo Reyes, David Depew, Theresa Santos, Cheryl Jovillar, Peejay the Great, Ivan Avina, Lindsey Wagner, Carlos Crouse, Frank Young, and Katerina Mellos. None of you are African but you sang to me universal tunes of kindness, care, and scholarship. If I ever meet God, I'll tell Him I know you.

Even on one's deathbed, one always breathes the hope of living and planning. For down deep into my entermost being of being, I never entertained death or dying; even remotely. I thought I was a rock. My self-delusions was however, punctured wide open one day, when my younger brother, Dr. Shalewa Olafioye, called to inform me that my eldest child, Solape, had been drenching herself in a rain of tears over me. Many members of our family shared her fears. They saw in me, felt in my voice, and smelt in me, what I did not. Those who were close to my daughter, could not stem her torrents. Suddenly, it hit me, the possibility of it, that I might not make it. Sometimes illness is a betrayal. The thought of it, that some people so genuinely cared, touched me so intuitively and inmostly. I never knew that my life could be so deeply impact their own. I am truly, very grateful. To all my relatives, young and old, brothers and sisters, you all know how I feel about your inner turmoils and anguishes. Life is a preparation for death but my inner thoughts are on survival even though I have nothing but books to bequest.

Jumoke Okoya-Olafioye wears the head gear of honor and the heart of a lion. She is my youngest brother's – Tunde Olafioye's wife in London. I have never met her. Despite the rigors of her studies at the University of East London – Masters in Business Information System – she still finds the time to e-mail me or send me a card every week asking after my health; with prayers. That's all she has. How do you refund such a goodness!! Leave it to the galaxy of deities. They see every heart.

Foreword

The biography of my illness

– Tayo Olafioye

This year or season has been horrible, the weather of my health, inclement. That I live to write about it, is my celebration and therapy. Not often does a writer make public the confessional state of his or her health. The only thing to prove is that, at times, it is possible to survive the collective interventions of expertly care, manifold beatitudes, tailored living, inestimable luck and ancestral fortifications. They refuse to condone any of my bouts with cyclonic daze. Many have succumbed to lesser travails.

Stage I

It started in a week when incontinence visited me; frequent urination, that is. My Yoruba cultural background would probably have dubbed it. "a-to-gbe," an attack of urinary dehydration. By mid-week, I made it to the hospital for investigation, at the Kaiser Permanente Hospital on Zion in San Diego, California. The doctor demanded a urine specimen which the laboratory analyzed with immediacy.

The doctor, Nathaniel Nitahar, suspected an enlarged prostate. "What is that?" I snapped. "I have never heard of it." "Don't worry," the doctor consoled. "Let's find out first." The nurse motioned me to enter a privacy to disrobe and put on a hospital garment with a split back. I did as ordered. I was led to a theatre adorned with medical gadgets and lights. I was asked to lie on a long table, padded nice and clean with a calico sheet. "The doctor will soon be with you," the assistant offered.

The doctor soon arrived and he introduced his retinue of medical nerds[1]. They spoke soothingly as if to calm my frayed nerves. I had no idea what to expect. Every member of the team dressed in green hospital garbs. They wore gloves and half masks to entertain their nostrils and mouths. The doctor told me what to anticipate but I had no practical, or mental inkling of what he meant. I lazily understood him. He proceeded to introduce my behind by yanking it to the cold air with an open space before everyone's prying eyes. I felt violated but who was I to squawk before death? The doctor showed me a thin, long, steel, brass, stick or baton, supposedly a camera that violated my internal organs. The doctor gently guided it on an investigative tour of my inside from the entry gate of my behind. Suddenly, I heard a click and a sharp bite from within. This thing was eating my flesh and drinking my blood as its beverage. " Be calm," the doctor consoled. "Seven more bites and we will be through." There is no hidden hand without a hidden fist. The team was watching my inside on the monitor all along. This was the beginning of my ordeals.

Days later, the doctor announced that this tomato size object called prostate was very large and must be removed shortly after, a second investigation. If not, it would turn cancerous. It had been pressing on my urinary tract, hence the incontinence.

No sooner than that when I received a call, that the doctor needed me to visit him without delay. "You have a choice," the doctor announced. "You can let the prostate grow bigger and bigger and let it turn deadly cancerous, or we remove it now with some risks." "What risks?" I inquired timidly. The doctor replied, "Well, we cannot guarantee that the lines of your

---

[1] Nerds – Geniuses

sexual function will remain. Doctors make mistakes. We may not be able to save it."

Some cold shivered down my spine. I have really had it, I thought. "But my wife is still young." I protested. "I understand that" the doctor said endearingly. "It is not definitive that this scenario will play out but we must let you know, just in case. Why don't you think about it and read lots of literature on prostate. Talk to people. Seek other opinions and let me hear from you soon so that we can schedule a date for the surgery. It is very urgent. We may be lucky to arrest a lot of unpleasantness now."

I was bemused, confused and dazed. In one stretch, my life seemed at an end. A storm was gathering before my eyes. There was no telling what devastation it would cause. I concluded that I would lose my family life. This was a living torture, an emotional inferno and mostly psychological death. I raced to a precipitate bonfire of conclusions. It was all over, I professed. What a laughing stock I would become. What a toothless bulldog stalking the street!. A stallion without stamina! What a state of psychological vacuity! You want to know that it is there, if you need it or that you are complete even if you do not need the weapon from your arsenal.

I summoned courage to call my old reliables to know more about the disease. "You will be fine," re-assured Dr John Olowoyeye, a cardiologist in northern California. We were contemporaries at the grammar school called, Christ's School, Ado-Ekiti in Western Nigeria.

"I believe in prayers," counseled my cousin, Dr Oke Ibitoye who practices medicine in Maryland. From his base in Station Island in New York, another cousin, Dr. Odimayo Akindutire declared, " Nothing is beyond the reach of the Almighty. His long healing hand can reach all nooks and corners. There is no need to panic." Both doctors gave calls to Dr Nitahar, the surgeon in charge. They made their own inquiries. My little brother, Dr Shalewa Olafioye, an AIDS expert, was not fazed by my commotion. "Big fellow, I advise that you listen to your doctor. I would love to know more of the history in your condition."

We had the surgery. All the poems about it are the speaking pictures of my experience. I did almost a week in the hospital. Dr Nitahara, as the head surgeon of my ordeal, made his rounds quite often. He told the family that all went well. My mother-in-law was with us at the time. The doctor intimated that all the offending diseases were removed and stated: "The prostate was gone and no cancer of any type lingers around. We need to monitor you for sometime to come. In addition to everything else, I am happy to inform you that you are a full man. Nothing was cut. Your manly functions remained intact, you should be pleased to know." I responded, "Yes, I am. Even if I do not use my instrument, it is satisfying to know that it is there. I already felt its movement."

"Yes, it is called an erection, you suffer no erectal dysfunction at all. I noticed that you did not take your pain medication. You endured those terrible pains. You are a very brave man," said the doctor. "The pains were severe, doctor. I got used to them. So, I held out without medication. I tried to ignore the pain. May be I am crazy," I said.

When a sick person is maturing to a candidacy in expiration, the family practices a cover-up of the nature of illness. If he or she were eminent, society practices media speculation and denials from spokes-persons. They claim in the lingo of the sophisticated - - privacy. The irony is that when the candidate eventually kicks the bucket, the silly cat will jump out of the bag and assume a life of its own. Worse still, traditional societies swing to wide extremes. They read diabolics into the affliction. Everyone suspects the other in the family as the errant witch or wizard. All nocturnal movements, or proverbial ditties, are placed under the umbrella of suspicion. The head co-wife, in a polygamous setting, becomes hunted by the husband's relatives. So also is any of the other wives. An innocent or bitter relative, distant or near, could be in jeopardy. Family quarrels of eons ago could be re-visited for dirt in the dung-heap, or any troublesome co-worker could stand accused, however innocent or cosmopolitan. A bird flying at night and chirping is misconstrued as heading for a convention of witches. No evidence to prove anything but a giddy, cultural festival of inquisition pervades.

At another level, however Christian or Islamic, some family members, in desperation can consult prophets, traditional medicants, shamans, native or witch doctors, and fortune tellers, ad infinitum. Valuable, scanty family resources are expended on procuring goats, rams or cows, herbs accompanied with sacrificial chants to placate ancestors, spiritual pantheons and also to ward off perceived or imagined enemies. All these may not have anything to do with the biology of the disease in question, though one must grant that some genuine traditional medications or fortifications do work in some instances.

During the tense moments of my pestilence, some literary colleagues got wind of my situation. You cannot seal it up in a jar forever, however hermitically. It will bubble to the surface. Many called when I was at the hospital. Others called the family at home, sometimes repeatedly. Such honorable mentions are due Tanure Ojaide (poet, critic), Charles Mann (Linguist and Critic), Isidore Okpewho (critic and novelist), Niyi Osundare (poet, critic), Rasheed Na'Allah (writer and critic), Bayo and Nike Lawal (statisticain; linguist), Odun Balogun (writer and critic), Ode Ogede (writer and critic), Sunday Babaoye (doctor), Dr Balogun Chike Obi (phycist), Femi Ojo-ade (French specialist and critic), and Dr (Mrs) Ugonna Chike Obi (neonatologist).

Stage II

While I was recovering from the first affliction, a silent but potent expeditionary force assailed and ambushed me. I woke up one morning in the summer of 99 and went to the bathroom to clean up for school. The room twirled and appeared upside down. I staggered and could not maintain my balance. My head spun and was shaking. I must be having vertigo. So I thought. What hell is this O God! Is this the beginning of the end! So I exasperated. I could not lift my right hand to brush my teeth. It was stiff. I could not comb my hair nor tie the strings of my shoes. I managed after several attempts to dress up and drove to school. Driving became a tug of war. While I meant to stay within the lane, my head would order the car to move to the right in a possible calamitous collision with cars plying on the right. I sweated profusely to make it to school. I did not last the next three hours. A friend drove me to meet my doctor, some thirty miles away from school. Alas, it was my doctor's day off—Dr Robert Felder, a very nice special man in my life, at Kaiser Hospital in Carlsbad, California. A young-female-tendril primary doctor examined me. "I think you have a TIA, Professor Tayo." "What's that?" I inquired ignorantly. "That is a stroke without a stroke. You are very lucky. It came and went away. Your face did not collapse. Your right side is only mildly affected. Your speech is very clear and strong, but I cannot allow you to go home. You must see a specialist right away for treatment." I was transferred to Palomar Hospital in Escondido, a few kilometers away. My family heard from the hospital at 10pm, I was hospitalized. Here I remained for the next four days. Dr Felder and associates paraded to my room almost daily. I received blood thinners, did MRI's at the Imaging Institute, and got better and finally walked again. I received instructions in physical therapy, diet and exercises. I went home. The hospital arranged my transportation.

Days later, Dr Jay Rosenberg, the neurology consultant at Kaiser Zion, near my home in Old Town, San Diego called. I went to see him. The man is a breathing encyclopedia of medical linguistics. He examined me and talked in rapid monologues as he recorded himself on the computer. I was animated with him. He won my heart. He was vertical and adept with language and knowledge of medicine. He was dynamic and sharp. I became his disciple without hesitation.

"Tayo, what is going on here? You are still a young man, and you have been through so much already this year. I am glad to see you, still smiling. That's character." He made his recommendation that Dr David Levy, the Neurosurgeon should see me for the next stage, Dr. Levy then recommended a brain surgery procedure if cerebral angiogram confirmed their suspicion. The offending artery must be dilated to permit blood to flow. "The procedure is called stenting, and it is very risky. If we are lucky, it can be conveniently done. We will put a balloon into one the narrowing one of the important arteries that go to the brain, to open it up, just as we do to the heart. You will be under observation for the next 48 hours in the hospital after surgery."

Appointments were made. I went for the arteriogram on the 12th of October 1999. Some poems will attest to that encounter in this collection. I stayed in the hospital for almost eight hours. My cousin, Martin, followed me to and from the hospital. Soon after arriving there, I was asked to disrobe to my birthday suit and wear a nameless hospital garment. A bed awaited me. There I lay and received an intravenous line. Soon I made it to the theater of "Special procedures" or something to that effect. The gadgetry in there shook my confidence a little, seeing very large cauldron sized cameras and monitors and a miscellaneous assortment of instruments. I was transferred to a special bed with a tiny forked headrest. They held down my head with tape. My entire body was covered with very heavy cellophane drapes. They covered my nose with an oxygen belching tube. It was a smoke screen for something else. I must have been asleep for the following two hours without knowing it. I forgot everything. They had incised the femoral artery in the groin in my sleep without pain. My groin area had been shaved. I located the spot of incision through which they fed their dye, the next morning. When I woke up from the surgery, they took X-ray pictures galore. They rattled commands to make sure perhaps, that I was still breathing. The X-ray demanded it.

I felt groggy. My head was woozy. I had planned to teach at the National University that evening. The doctor vetoed me. My legs could hardly carry me. The evening closed in and Martin was permitted to ship me home. I slumped onto our living room couch. There I slept till 2:45am when my daughter tiptoed in to wake me up.

"Daddy, why aren't you in your bed? I am cold. Cover me up in my room." I trudged and thrashed around to fetch her an additional blanket. I enjoy doing those family chores for my child.

My wife believes in God and the hospital, especially Dr Felder, our friend. That's the extent of her concerns. Femi, my daughter mused aloud, "Daddy, please don't die. God will take care of you. If something happens to you, I would have nobody to trust and feel free to tell my secrets", usually, primary school rascalities.

My Dean, Renee Kilmer at Southwestern, was always kind to me. I had no trouble getting permission for my hospital visits or getting sponsored for conferences. Bertha, our gorgeous black secretary with her Hispanic counterparts, Mariana calls me "Africa" endearingly, and they closely monitored my delicacy with soothing inquiries. Jane Tassi, a sectional head of our Department Computer Services is an angel. You have the impression that she is a feminist and an intellectual in her own right. She is enormously warm and gentle with me. Always concerned and worried. She brought me her late father's walking stick to steady my gait. I will never forget any of them. They touched me with their enormous humanity. Some Americans are so very special.

Stage III

In the evening of Friday the 15th of October, 1999. Dr David Levy called and said: "Tayo, I have examined the film of your cerebral angiogram. You have a stenosis in the brain—a narrowing of the artery. Surgery is the only way to go, if we are to arrest the problem on time. I have consulted with many experts and we all agreed that surgery is the best choice. The prospect looks very good for your kind of condition. We have done 15 to date. The procedure as you know, is called angioplasty stenting. The surgery will take place in New York. You and I will fly to New York where they are preparing for us, if you agree with our assessment. There are other experts waiting for us there. The hospital will take care of everything. You will stay behind for a day or two for observation before you fly back to San Diego. I will fly back here immediately after the surgery. We are planning to leave here on Sunday, the 5th of December. Early Monday morning of the following day, the operation will take place. Please get back in touch with me as soon as possible, having done all the consultations, you may need."

"Thank you, doctor. I am very excited at this prospect, risky as it is. As we say back home, the goat will finally kill this leopard."

"We'll keep our fingers crossed. All things being equal, we are good and confident. Bye for now."

Dr Ugonna Chike Obi, a very good friend of my wife, and also the wife of a colleague advised her to ask me to call Dr. Bola Oyeshiku, a Nigerian neurosurgeon, in Atlanta for an additional opinion. The Doctor called Dr. Levy. They both agreed that the surgery was most vital and urgent.

A new twist develops as my World turns:

"Gring! Gring!" the phone rang.
"Hello"
"Dr. Levy here."
"What's up Doc?"

I was a bit apprehensive because the surgery in New York had been postponed once. We had the 27th of December yet to be confirmed, but some days later the 13th was chosen to be suitable. On this present call, the news was ominous, only for a minute. Dr. Levy did not allow its impact to register.

"Tayo, Buffalo turned us down. They would not give us their cooperation as planned."

"But why doctor?"

"They are afraid that the surgery is too complicated. The artery blocked in the brain is too curvy to be reached. You know what? There is also good news. I only wanted their collaboration since this procedure is relatively new. But as heavens would have it, I am ahead of them in the experience of treating this problem. I am confident that despite all the risks, we can safely get you through here in San Diego. The technology I'll use for you is far superior to theirs, which they were going to use for you. I'll go ahead and order the superior technology and instruments. We have many options, so I am going to consult my colleagues for their views. We will meet again soon after arrangements are made. We'll then schedule the surgery. We have the option of a bypass, but that may not be necessary. All operations are risky. I am confident, however, of our expertise, so don't worry. We don't need New York at all. When does school start for you? After Christmas?"

"January 10th."

"That is good. Plenty of time to recover."

"Thank you doctor, I leave it all to you. You have been kind and concerned with me, and I cannot ask for more. I am lucky to be receiving this attention. After all, you have no intention to kill me or maim my health. I am eternally grateful."

"We are here for you. See you soon."

I shed a few private tears as the doctor dropped the phone. I was hurt that New York thought me a basket case. If that were so, they would've abandoned me to the throes of precipitate and imminent death, if I were their resident patient in Buffalo. As my doctor said, "There is a great blessing sometimes behind every disappointment. I can now do that which I do best."

As I calmed down, I hardly knew when I composed the work below. I typed it and took it to the notary to notarize and distribute copies, except my wife's copy, which I'll hold until the moment of my departure. I enveloped it and placed it on her table with a note of thanks for all the years- just in case I never have any other opportunity to say "I love and appreciate you."

Brain surgery

To my wife, children, and family at-large...
    If anything were to happen to me during this procedure, or there after, please do not sue or exploit the kindness of Dr. David Levy and his team or the Kaiser establishment. While Buffalo turned us down amidst this turbulence in the sea of life, Dr. Levy, despite the risks, is courageous to put his expertise on the line to help me. He meant well and this I appreciate beyond reprieve. He should not suffer reprisals or disrepute for his altruism. Besides, he will do his utmost to achieve a fair result. May the heavens and my ancestors help him. David, do all you can to help my family, just in case...especially my daughter who is only ten. Dr. Nitahari, Urology, Kaiser, Otay Mesa and I, had once discussed her education at the University of California San Diego, my alma mater. He is interested in her. Team up with him, please, to organize something for her future, if it needs to be. Thanks to you all.

Tayo Olafioye, Ph.D.
November 28, 1999

A personal note to my wife:

I want to thank you from the bottom of my heart for all the years. While you were asleep or busy quarreling and giving me the silent treatment, sometimes my tears were busy silently standing on my pillow. This might be our last togetherness. I thank you for your devotion and courage. I never can tell what tomorrow will bring in this situation. Take care of our child, Femi. I love you all. It had been a very jolly ride. My immense and immeasurable gratitude.

    Eternally,
    Tayo

The saga continues in this diary of events

By 1 p.m. this Wednesday, the 30th of November, Dr. David Levy gave me a call. The twist continued. He had met his departmental consultative assembly of medic-nerds on my case specifically.

"They counseled further tests." He announced. "And we agreed to take it easy because this is a very risky undertaking. Dr. Jay Rosenberg was there. The doctors said that we should refer you to see our cardiologist, to ensure the healthy functioning of you heart before we proceed. Might there be a problem to be discovered anew. We even considered alternative medication to surgery if it would help alleviate your condition. We want to do the best for you. If your heart poses no problem, we may end up doing the operation. But let's attend to unexpected problems now. For further necessary investigation, I'll want you to see me and also Dr. Rosenburg. You will hear from the cardiologist's nurse within a week. If they are late calling you, give me a call so that we urge them to expedite. I'll ask my nurse to make arrangements for you to see me. You are fine for now. It takes a long time for the artery to narrow further. Let's take care of possible obstacles first, O.K.? See you soon."

After a few minutes of a sweaty rush through my pores, I realized that I am really very lucky. All these experts are treading slowly to not make any mistakes on me, I was neither depressed nor anguished. Any fatal blow may be irretrievable. Caution is the anthem, they know but I don't know what they do know. I booked an appointment with Rosenburg for the following days. Come to think of it, maybe Buffalo was right after all. Time will tell.

Dunni, one of my siblings, never wanted this surgery. She was weepingly vociferous against it.

"Oh no brother!" She anguished. She committed the matter to prayer, as did many other relatives.

"I'm not in a hurry to die, far from it. I feel the spiritual universe is watching over me. For the moment however, I am between a rock and a hard place. There is no escape from this reality. I am truly in the eye of the storm. Only a survivor knows 'the burden'."

October 19, 1999

To Whom It May Concern:

Tayo Olafioye has been under my medical care since early this calendar year. In March he underwent extensive surgery for the treatment of prostrate. Since his surgery, he has endured the routine postoperative changes, which have necessitated that he not work for 6 weeks from the time of surgery. In addition, he has needed the prolonged use of multiple medications. Mister Olafioye will need continued medical monitoring at regular intervals to assess his progress from the time of surgery.

Kenneth Nitahara, MD
Kaiser Permanente, San Diego

I kept my appointment with Dr. Rosenberg. He did not mince a word. His objection was uncompromising. He viewed surgery dimly. "The brain is the engine room of the body. To tinker with it, is to invite what you were trying to prevent. The blocked artery is right inside your brain, the ravine of it. If you were my son, I would be hesitant. Caution first, clarity second. Even if your heart were sound, I'll still object. Dr. Levy and I have agreed in conference to treat you by other means. Not this risky operation." His submission virtually killed the enthusiasm. And now, everybody believes their unspoken anxieties.

In time, this cyclone will pass and it will be history. I look forward to an effective treatment, so that life can be full and jolly again. One never truly knows how golden life is until one squeezes through the eye of the needle. Those who die peacefully or instantly, without the pestilence or ravages of infirmities in their chambers, owe a trillion gratitudes to death. They never see their lives ebb before them. They never have to struggle to breathe. They never suffer the agonies of excruciating discomfort. They never see their loved ones and friends whittle in agony, helplessly within, for their sake. Nobody dies alone.

*Note: Today, Friday, the 10th of December 1999, my brain surgery was officially postponed for four months, at least to give all contesting approaches and proprieties time to breathe. The doctors held their departmental conference on me (consultation really in other cultures' medical tradition). They arranged their cardiologist to examine my heart. Thoroughly, they scheduled older patients with similar conditions or prognosis, to blaze the procedure first before my turn. Thus the various surgical teams can assess their successes, failures or handicaps. Each consultant signaled active caution. I am very thrilled for it beyond imaginable measures. What the heck! You only live once. I am enjoying all the fuss over me. The doctors met with me after their conference. I was told that for the time being, I must stay on my various medications. The matter must be resolved. It cannot dangle forever like a plant without roots. I cannot manage any more disaster. There is a limit to human endurance.

My book as a stroke of hope is a metaphor. Double, triple or quadriple entendre. It hits at many levels of meanings and interpretations. It was a stroke of discovery that my affliction was caught at its very early stage, gathering siesmic tremor to explode. It was a stroke of celestial determination that I ran into Kaiser's expert physicians who care.

They refused to count me a statistic of waste, which was a stroke of providential and ancestral interposition. My stroke was mild, thereby providing me the chance to fully recover. Many are not so lucky. I do not dangle in spacey unreality without roots or diminished capacity as a human being, a carcass of my former vibrancy. I could have been six feet under. It was a stroke of luck that all elements converged to make life worthy. It was a stroke of fate, an accident of hope, that I have a second chance. To die a hero or a martyr is meaningless. Life is my hope. Hope is my future. I must take care of it because I must be there. This smack, a stroke of survival and retrieval not helplessness hopelessness or hopeless helplessness.

The concept of a stroke that incapacitates or destroys, being a subject of speculative hope, is in itself an irony, possibly an oxymoron as well. This is my paradox; my eloquent dilemma.

Current Medical Advance in the USA

David Levy, M.D.
Department of Neurosurgery, Kaiser Permanente.
San Diego; California.

Re: Tayo Olafioye

Tayo Olafioye is a fifty-five year old right handed Nigerian English professor who developed episodes of balance difficulties, weakness and numbness of his right arm and leg in June, 1999. This resulted in some difficulty walking. Within two weeks, his motor function and ability to walk had returned but not to its full capacity. His right arm function has not yet fully returned. He developed fatigue easily but has further episodes of weakness or numbness since June 1999. He was placed on blood thinners since that time. On examination, he appears to have good strength in both lower extremities and he walks without difficulty.

When I first met Tayo Olafioye, he was obviously a kind and gentle man. At his relatively young age for these medical problems, he was coping well with difficulty. His studies included an MR angiography, which demonstrated a high grade narrowing of his left middle artery which corresponds to the area of the stroke. It was obvious that he had some residual weakness of his right arm, thus signaling some neuronal depth in the region of the left middle cerebral artery. The angiogram demonstrated the narrowing was significant.

There has been a movement recently to treat patients with high grade stenosis of their intracranial arteries with angioplasty and, most recently, intracranial stenting. An intracranial stent is a slotted tube that can be expanded once it is inside a narrowing. It is expanded using a balloon which expands the artery and narrowing, while the stent, once expanded, does not allow the artery to contract again, keeping the stenosis open and allowing greater blood flow through the stenosis. There is currently no intracranial stent that is FDA approved. However, there is one stent specifically designed for intracranial vessels that is currently in trials in Buffalo, New York, under the direction of Dr. L.N. Hopkins.

I presented Dr. Olafioye with the options that included treating this with blood thinning medication, which he would need to stay on for the remainder of his life, or an attempt at intracranial stent placement. The procedure is a new procedure and, thus, the risks are not fully known. The experience we have with angioplasty and stenting in the arteries of the heart as well in other arteries in the body generally yields good results, however, given the fact that the arteries of the brain are so small and so thin walled, a separate trial is necessary. Therefore, with Dr. Olafioye's approval and with his full understanding of the risks involved in undertaking such treatment, we will plan to fly to Buffalo, New York to attempt to place a stent in the middle left middle cerebral artery. At this time, it is not known if, with his tortuous anatomy, we will be able to even bring the device to the area of narrowing. However, an attempt will be made.

A poet facing life, death and posterity

Often, perhaps too often, we forget that certain people – professionals, professors, poets – are mere mortals, like the rest of us, doomed to fall victim to that implacable grandmaster of destruction, Death. However, what distinguishes a handful of individuals from the vast majority is, the quality of life, the determination to defy death, to stand up and shout a resounding No! No, to cowardice. No, to connivance. No, to corruption. For, these acts and attitudes of revolt, nay, of revolution, are not posited in isolation; they are symbolic of an overall philosophy encompassing everything that comes together in the complex whole called Life. Life, not everlasting, but short, of a season. Life, potentially innocent, sweet, marked by moral rectitude, and a consciousness of, as well as a commitment to, values that lift humanity to the zenith of achievement and accomplishment. Yet, Life, dragged down to the depths of disease and destruction by locusts and vampires and vultures disguised as humans. And, the real human beings are compelled to choose between the condition of slaves, victims of those doctors of death, and the status of the courageous, revolutionaries fighting for freedom, and prepared to pay the ultimate price so that they, by all means necessary, may become immortals in the annals of posterity. A contradiction in terms, one can hear some cynics sneer through their yellow teeth - a sure sign of cowardice!

Those that are fortunate to read *A Stroke of Hope* will have a ready answer for such nay sayers. Here is a poet, a mere mortal, doing something strange: He reveals to his audience his innermost thoughts, at that instant when most would prefer to keep their secrets secret; when they would rather guard their privacy jealously and obsessively, in order not to reveal their deficiencies, in order not to tumble down from their heights of hypocrisy and ego-tripping. And, this poet goes farther, by making of his audience, at first, reluctant companions in his journey through existential hell; and then, with his poetic skills of making magic with words and striking the chord of communality well learnt from his African culture, winning over his audience to share in his escape from that hell to the point where, together, they can look death in the eye, with defiance, but not absolutely, not with the demonic demeanor of dictators so common to his ancestral continent. In a word, Tayo Olafioye's poems reveal his thoughts, his fears and despair, in the midst of his season of "stroke without a stroke;" his doubts, as to whether he would survive the onslaught, or succumb; his rising courage, and (almost) conviction, that is, the hope, that he will not die, because he has too much to live for. Family, Friends, Students, and Society, the society that is the human universe but, precisely, that society that begins and ends in his Africa; for Tayo knows full well that he is "always an African at heart." (MY EPITAPH WHENEVER)

A particularly striking aspect of the collection is the preamble to the poetry, where the poet presents the biography of his illness, and the reviews of the three doctor-surgeons engaged in his care. As already affirmed, one's first reaction might be, that this is strange, too strange to behold. Nonetheless, without this introduction, one cannot fully comprehend the poems. The introductory details set the stage, as it were, or, indeed, provide the surface existential panorama, for the drama that unfolds in the poems. Those descriptions of the patient's condition -fears, hopes, hopelessness, faith and, especially, love at the edge of the abyss- allow us to empathize with the patient-poet, to share in his story, and conclude, as he does, that "whoever has not died does not know the joy of living."

The body of poems is divided into four parts, each identified with a hospital room, and a major theme. The first is, "Room 211 - On Illness." The poems here are the most intimate and excruciating of all, being the most central to the patient's condition, and the most personal to him and his psyche. His reactions to the surgeons' opinions and actions. His contemplation of pain in all its ramifications, and the professionalism of his doctors. Most importantly, the journey from Life, to the gates of Death, and back. "I am not in a hurry to die, far from it. I feel the spiritual universe is watching over me," the poet confirms to a sibling totally scared and opposed to surgery. That determination to live is aided and, indeed, encouraged and pushed to the fore by the surgeons, "super gods," and "wizards":

> Without them
> Where shall we be?

As he does in quite a number of poems in the collection, Tayo uses the format of dichotomy and contrast to examine and explore the constant struggle to survive. While surgeons symbolize survival, the earthen soil represents the force of control and destruction:

> Never sick
> But devours daily, in sumptuous gulps.
> (SURGEONS)

Metaphor is also a constant. Cancer is "the stealth bomber of the physique," to whom the poet pays homage, reluctantly and ironically. "To know [prostate cancer] is to smell death." In the poem, THE MECHANICS OF PHYSIQUE, Tayo describes himself as

> the guest of ill health
> in the home of repairs.

The "home" could be one of healing, but also one of the horror of death. Hence, while praising the surgeons, the poet does not eschew the presence of the murderous Enemy, Death. LET ME TROT AGAIN finds him at the crossroads between Life and Death, ready to go under the *knife*, the same instrument used in carving up a chicken and in cutting out cancer from the human body. Thus, one is struck by the inextricable link between life and death.

Then, Hope begins to loom large.

> I hope to listen
> To the sounds of paradise
> If I make it there.

Would that mean that the patient is prepared to quit this vale of tears, and soar to life everlasting in the great beyond? One finds references to religion spread through the pages of this collection. Happily that those are passing moments, surpassed by others that declare hope in life, this life, here and now. Such hope is expressed in the poem, AT THE MOMENT OF DEPARTURE, dedicated to the poet's daughter, and in the poems written for his three surgeons. THE POETRY OF DEATH admits the finality of life, but without resigning himself to that fate.

In the surgeon poems, there are metaphors galore, expressing and emphasizing the strengths of those individuals fighting death to the finish.

> *You are the tiger who strides stealthily*
> *Not of cowardice*
> *But of knowledge of the landscape.*

Such usage of animals -a reference point for Tayo's Africanity- abounds in the text. Tigers, elephants, lions, as well as myths and legends, and deities, come up as a reminder of the wisdom of a culture much maligned by the western masters. PRAYER is proof of the viability of African culture, and religion. Just as "genius knows no color or race," so does religion refuse to categorize any cult as superior to others.

That remark brings us to Part Two of the book, "Room 34 - Nigerian Condition." The question would be, how come a patient combating death, would be thinking of some faraway place called Nigeria, when he should be using all his energy -physical and psychological- to fight his own battle? The response is a no-brainer for the committed artist: Victory in the personal battle can only be meaningful in the knowledge that the sickness of the Nigerian (his home) society is extracted, like cancer! For, the reality of Nigeria is reason enough to fall sick. The country, reputedly "giant of Africa," has been reduced to the stature of a gnome by dictator Abacha, "a veritable evil," "the Khalif of ritual death," and his horde of "moral lepers," "cancer-invalids," mired in criminality, corruption, greed, and graft, and "the arrogance of invincibility." This feeling of immortality subtly links the second section to the first; only, of course, while the poet recognizes his human frailty as he struggles to survive the onslaught of Death, these nitwits misruling a country turned into their serfdom, know no reason to stench their megalomania. But, unlike the poet, a survivor, Abacha, an anti-Christ figure "never made to walk on water," is suddenly cut down by Death: "God's true coup silenced the beast." Furthermore, the hope fitfully explored in the first part of the collection, now comes into full bloom. "Hope breathes new life," the poet exalts.

Today is resurrection and retrieval
The people bellow their hallelujahs.

Nonetheless, just as the patient cannot forget that his struggle is a continuous process, so also are the people of Nigeria cautioned: DO NOT FORGET. Even with the coronation of a new civilian (once military) president who vows to eradicate corruption in the land, the poet maintains a wait-and-see attitude. THEY START AGAIN recounts the parliamentarians' decadent behavior (can a tiger change its spots?). The poet-turned-doctor prescribes for sick Nigeria: "service without pay."

The country, terribly sick and comatose
In the hospital of anomie
Needs all medications of cure.

From the Nigerian patient, we move to Part Three, "Room 406 - International Scene." Here, evil also prevails, although the profundity does not approach that exemplified by Nigeria. FACES OF INFAMY, with a refrain reminiscent of African orature's call and response, lists various scenes of human sickness, "where [reign] hopelessness, a helplessness forgetfulness a death." Death is a Presence, with the disappearance of some famous ones (THE SUN ALSO SETS IN CAMELOT, about the death of John Kennedy, Jr.) reminding us that the Enemy knows no class. Which does not diminish the madness of ego-trippers carrying stone in place of a heart (THE CUBISM OF MAYHEM). But all is not lost, as we read MANDELA... Yet, one wonders whether bidding good-bye to the noble man, "the tallest tree in Africa," "the most courageous of this millennium," and witnessing the end of "this millennium of pains," would at once mean the end of all our sufferings in Africa.

The final section, "Room 512 - Cultural Garden," proffers one possibility for rehabilitating Africa's humanity, through Culture. IWO FESTIVALS, with poetic dexterity and a humor rare in the collection, recounts the triumph of Yoruba culture over Christianity. The pastor of Ilutitun (Yoruba: new city), symbol of modernity, "a western civilized idiot," leads unwary women to their doom when they are urged to disobey age-old laws of traditional religion. In this section, Tayo makes quite a number of thought-provoking statements, mostly anchored on the wisdom of his culture. "Any society without myth or festival is dead." (IWO FESTIVALS)

Nobody needs reality
More than those
Who have none to give.
(OH! NO! MY SON BECOMES A GIRL!)
It makes no difference
If a man sees a snake
And a woman kills it. (Ibid.)

Pronouncements of human values based upon quality of character, viability of culture, and non-sexism, they express a position already found in Tayo's published writings. The question of women's condition would, no doubt, interest many a western reader. Caution: No Eurocentric feminism in this poetry; rather, there is an African humanism underscoring each gender's qualities and roles, and the ultimate complementarity within the totality of existential and experiential firmament. Thus, the poet, as a father, is not ashamed to fawn upon his beautiful little girl; nor is he hesitant to draw a portrait of his wife and her knack for disguise and mystery. The image of complementarity is marvelously captured in KAMA KEVIN KING, in which a black couple (king and queen) raises their "son of the gods," a continuity of their shared nobility.

The poem, ISLANDS OF SPIRITS IN AFRICAN COSMOS, depicts our pantheons and deities,
Creative or destructive

Blessings or a cure
Demons or gods.

In paying homage to these spirits, the poet returns to the beginning of his journey, to once again raise the essential questions about Life and Death. The difference now is, that he has conquered fear, and hopelessness.

The original title of the book was, *My Season of Inconvenience*. Upon reading the text, one is convinced of the superiority of the new title. The poetry itself constitutes a *stroke*, as "of the pen," or, of the artist's brush, putting down on paper feelings and ideas that bear an important message for the community. *Stroke*, too, as regards a sudden occurrence, as "of luck," reminding us that the poet is fortunate to be here with us, as we are to be in a position to read these soul-searching verses. And, of course, *stroke*, as that never expected stoppage, and seizure, of bodily functions, immobilizing all motors, transforming an active man into a static and stagnant liability. When combined with *hope*, the picture becomes complex, but comprehensive, and complete, as human life, before the dreaded Death.

A word about the genesis of this essay. When Tayo contacted me to do it, I sensed in his voice a certain urgency, a certain desperation. I hesitated to accept. Maybe out of a formless fear. Maybe due to the desire to keep a safe distance from things treating Death. Maybe out of a certain cowardice. But, then, I thought more about it all. We met only a couple of years ago, but have known each other for much longer, through our works, as critics and creative artists born and bred in the same sick society; as victims of oppressors in a system suffocating and stifling life, and desirous of destroying its own children; and as survivors refusing to quit the struggle.

So, I ended up accepting to write the essay. Now that I have read the text, and written the above, from the heart, I feel blessed, and gratified. My sensitivity has been refueled (and let us hope the pumps in our dear Nigeria never again go dry!) and, I daresay, my life has been given more meaning, even as I know categorically that we all must die one day. That is our destiny. Fortunately for Tayo, the poet, the work, concrete, constructed in a language all his own, with heart and soul, will live for posterity.

Thank you, Tayo. *Ire o.*

Femi Ojo-Ade

Table of contents

Room 304 – Nigerian condition
Confessions of the moral lepers
Moral lepers - part II
Do not forget
Festivals of mayhem in the forest
The coronation of the elephant at Abuja
The smoke that thunders
They start again
This is our millennium
The black nemesis
The president rides *molue* (mini-bus)

Room 406 – International scene
Mandela – the tallest tree in Africa– retires
The faces of infamy
This island of graves
Speakers of dishonor
The graph of intelligence quotient
Peter Paul Wiplinger
Aujema
The cubism of mayhem
The sun also sets in Camelot
Y2k

Room 512 – Cultural garden
Iwo
Oh! No! My son becomes a girl!
Chess of the mind
Ancestors on trial
The logic of this life
Kama Kevin King
The alley cat
What is it?
Memorial ode: Mrs. Akintoye the princess
Islands of spirits in African cosmos

*Room numbers indicate the rooms in which I stayed
respectively during the various stages of my hospitalization.

Excerpts of inspiration & hope

I carry the sun within me
My nights are lit with the full moon
Every new day the dawn inspires me
I hear the birds chirping in unison with the waterfalls
Nature's chords of fidelity.

I spring briskly with my unseeing feet
My world fills with silence, the stillness of happiness.
My intimacy embraces distances from worries.
My heart works the miracles of the invincible.
I feel the presence of the unseen, and the
Hallelujah of resurrection

Who has not smelt death does not know the joy of
living.

---- ---- ---- ---- ---- ---- ---- ---- ---- ----

DO NOT forget
The season, mothers diluted
Oil, water, and salt only
As stew to feed their urchins
With yam and gari dough for supper.

DO NOT forget
When baked bread
From cassava tubers for breakfast
A very poisonous necessity to survive.

DO NOT forget
When it was fashionable for our women
To line the inside of their honey pots
With roles of cocaine
Only to retrieve for sale.

---- ---- ---- ---- ---- ---- ---- ---- ---- ---- ----

DO NOT forget
How we bastardized the rules of law.
We were demonized by monsters
Who grew hairs in their cavities
And mocked our ancestral beginnings.

HISTORY will carve the miscreant's names in blood.

Professor Olafioye – A dynamic and persistent individual

Professor Olafioye has been a constant and relentless pursuer of my input into his most recent work since the middle of December. On the way back from a recent meeting, I sat down and began to read his introduction to his work with fascination and thus began my journey of exploration into his world of poetry. Now you must understand that poetry has always been a foreign language to me and as everyone knows, Americans are "language dwarfs. I found my journey into Professor Olafioye's world a fascinating and exciting exploration of a land that I had previously perceived to be a jungle full of quick sand. My previous problem with poetry stemmed from a misunderstanding of a world I had interpreted as intellectually escaping reality. The words as painted by Professor Olafioye demonstrated to me how a real feeling state could be artistically presented as a written painting.

In medicine, we come into contact with individuals of wide and varied educational, economic, and cultural backgrounds with different ethical and religious beliefs. Having trained and practiced in a western cultural setting, it is a challenge to communicate with, educate and empower others who have different backgrounds to us. Dr. Olafioye, a native of Nigeria, presented to me for an opinion as to how he should approach his medical dilemma. Western medicine would like us to think tat the technological explosion of scientific discovery in the latter part of the twentieth and beginning of the twenty-first century has led to immortality with the ability to reverse all aspects of disease with little effort and no risk. He has diabetes that led to a stroke. He recovered and is highly functional. His evaluation revealed that he had a total occlusion of his carotid artery and had 60% narrowing of the other carotid within the circulation of the brain. This narrowing in one sense can be viewed as a time bomb waiting to cause its explosion of death and disability once it occludes. Any reasonable individual would look to reverse this narrowing and return to a steady state where no added risk of catastrophe exists.

At the present time, the issue is whether or not to undergo an experimental new procedure of passing a catheter into and dilating the blood vessel within the brain. Dr. Olafioye was willing to go for it! If this procedure could be done without any risk, Dr. Olafioye should go for it. However, the risk is that in the process of trying to prevent a disastrous stroke, there exists a considerable probability of inducing a catastrophic stroke in an individual who at this time is highly functional and the father of a 6 year-old. If we win we win big time but if we lose we lose gigantically! That is the dilemma and the responsibility of the neurologist to empower the patient to make the appropriate decision.

How do we learn to live with the unknown? Life is an adventure! Dr. Olafioye is living this adventure and through his poetry he translates this life adventure for all of us to enjoy. None of us knows how long our adventure will last or can predict when it will end. We wish for magic and miracles but unfortunately there is no magic and miracles are in short supply. Dr. Olafioye is a wiser individual for all that he has been through and his poetry expresses his true love for life's meaning.

Room 211

On Illness

Surgeons

Smart
Some think: as super gods
Maybe, super nerds
They are everything-
Without them
Where shall we be?
Only wizards talk diseases
Or strain blood.

This earthen-soil is never sick
But devours daily, in sumptuous gulps:
Earthquakes today,
Hurricanes tomorrow,
Volcano's viscosity,
Floods or tornadoes seasonally.
Its incubus promotes human terminations-
All, mincemeats in its rich esophagus.

It takes wizards to stem its pulls.
They can use a hatchet
To ease a fly
From a maladied head.

Tribute to the stealth bomber

Prostate-
The enemy of Eros
The god of Libido
The son of Aphrodite
Exponential potentate
Supreme power of evil
The prince of darkness
Phallic god unrefined,
Man's most dreaded scourge
Whose malevolent arrow- cancer
Shivers the spine
Most mortal males-
Mere mention alone:
Brands hot iron of fear
On the mind
I salute you!

To know you
Is to smell death.
Or asphyxiate the passages of life.
Silent attacks your mode.
Dry semen, your elixir.
Supreme power of evil
Malevolent prince of darkness
I salute you!
You renege attacks
Where fed-a-right
But they court
Your wrath and pestilence-
Those ignoramuses who offer
Tobacco, snuff, red meat, hot drinks
Carcinogenous beverages and such pollutants
Articles of unfilial hospitality
To your Most Dreaded Eminence-
Through gully channels of the esophagus

You hibernate in ambush
Fast- spreading your tentacles
In the streams of their veins-
Never to forgive
But to launch reprisals
You, the stealth bomber of the physique
I salute you-
Crown prince of decimation
Yes, almighty doctors-
Try to outwit your smartness:
They send their Chemo and radios
To repel your advance.
There you are-
Smiling in waiting,
Knowing, conquest is yours,
However long, the sanitary campaigns,
You will ravage everything-
The phallus and the hospitals
Mere shells of lives before.
But surely,
Physicians are the warriors of courage
They will assassinate your malevolence.

At that moment of departure

My nine-year-old was at school
I left her a note; my heart fell:

Good-bye my darling
As I go under the knife.
I pray to see you again
For which: I shall be grateful.
If not:
My time must have been done
I left you and mommy, phone numbers to call.
Remember always,
Daddy loves you to the end
And will never forget you.

You are the pupil
Of my eyes.
Our bond: no dictionary can define
Our blood: only Nature can refine
The language it speaks
Or the oneness it portends.

Fofo- my only one of history
Foyin-Femi- one who puts honey into my life
Good-bye for now,
I hope to see you again, soon
If Fate so designs.
The hunter who has only one arrow
Does not shoot aimlessly.

Let me trot again

I am on the road
Through the jagged paths of the unconscious,
Where forced to sleep
The stony lapse into no re-turn.
The knife, they say-
Not savory or jolly on the neck of a chicken,
If only I had a choice-
none of my own
As no line remains
In a sandstorm.

I hope to listen
To the sounds of paradise
If I make it there.
This jagged road to the unconscious,
The stony sleep into surgery.
Will I see the Christian light
At the end of the tunnel?
Or, simply the fellowship of sufferers?

This must be the research
Into the religion of death.
Maybe will be too leaden to care
If life exists on the other side-
Or simply, two worlds of disconnect?
These six hours of butchered sleep
In the landscaping of my abdomen.
The silent holocaust of my parts

I have taken a train
To the gate
Between life and death
To mind, a messy chore.

The moon that wanes today

Will be full tomorrow.
So God shooed me away-
Sinners like me.
His port was full, unprocessed.
"Not yet," my ancestors snapped.
Calmly, I turned to the resurrection
Of sleep-wake.
Confused and dazed:
"Where am I?" I sneered.
Arrogant again, you see! Forgetting that-
Life gives its own brand of justice.

Till then let me trot here for a little longer.

The poetry of death

Images of the mind:
Weird, nightly dreams-
Revolutions of the maimed,
Games that sickness plays
In the bed of discomfort.
Maybe not the bull,
But has got every horn
The bull employs.

Incisions and myriad tubes,
Bindings a-taut every stretch
All over the place.
Sometimes you wish as a candidate
Despair can be temporary
But the river must flow its course.
One must know
When one has pepper
In one's eyes

Tossing and turning
Groaning and moaning.
Dazed all night long
In formless imaginings
These are:
Many steps beyond the pale,
Bottles galore to drain
The catheters of inconvenience.

Only that some nurses are angels
Touch and voices are salvation,
To whiff the pains away.
He who is courteous
Is not a fool.
Illness, the great reminder of man's
Air-weight fragility.

When the time comes,
No man or fate can revise
The irrationality of death.

We try so vainly
To make our shadows dance
And the elephant to somersault
In the fiendish poetry of Death.
Or jig Ijala:[2]
The hunters' monodies of finality.

---

[2] Ijala- Hunters' traditional oral poetry

The mechanics of physique

I am the guest of ill health
In the home of repairs.
Moaning in silence
As the mechanics of physique
Salivate to vet their art on me.
We are many
Looking for tap roots
On the tree- tops of hope,
Each summarizing what life has meant.
Nothing matters now,
All the faces speak
The language of despair,
The outside is all – dark,
Prison without sun in our hearts,
This is the last stop
On our train ride
To success or failure,
Life or death,
Survival or hopelessness
Renaissance or life – of – no – return.
When the roots of a tree
Begin to decay
They spread death
To the branches
My mind was a messy grave
As I whispered good-bye to my family.
Here we were- passengers
Waiting to board the planes of ill health,
This surgical admitting room.
Our passports and papers stamped
Clipped, handed each for the guillotine.
To think this might be the last.
How this unknown paralyzed me
Such a moment of life's disconnect
A journey of no return.

An eerie feeling
I lay on the gurney at their command
Without clothes or fashion to impress
Just my birthday suit
For the mechanics to re- tool.

A fat lady trudged in
Kindly she was and professional
Introduced a liquid kiss to my vein,
That was the last I remembered.
Thus began in earnest
The prostate journey to death or renewal.
No C-word[3] or visitor in my mold
Told me in the wake after
Twenty-four hours of stony sleep.
"Where are we?" I asked
"When shall we do it?"
"Done since yesterday," the answer came
Some eyes stared over me
"We removed the large tomato
That pressed your channels.
Your sex nerves preserved.
Lucky you," the doctor enthused.

Soon I noticed, my chest oppressed
My tummy very leaden.
My head swam in cartoons of impossibilities
Nothing jelled in spacey unreality.
Three bottles and tubes labyrinth my nerves.
Drain as lifesavers.

Hats off to the nurses
Truly the angels of mercy.
Love patients and predicaments;
Master the dirty jobs,
No one else will be decent to do.

---

[3] C-word = cancer

I shall be home my chant
I shall be home my hope
Where I shall hug my special ones,
At the barnyard of survival,
The shrine of ancestral gratitude,
To live once again.
Home is the sweet return
From the wilds of ill heath.

Dr. Kenneth Nitahara
Kaiser, San Diego, California

Oracle, Mediciner, Diviner-
Size is no threat
To the labyrinth depths
Of your mind.
In the theatre of body mechanics
No Einstein can match your worth.
You are the tiger who strides stealthily,
Not of cowardice
But of knowledge of the landscape.
My surgeon- urologist, extra-ordinaire
A friend who tells your face
When your insides are ugly.

Moves smartly
To dike the corrosions of death.
Wherever possible, you safely
Rework the landscape
To save my breath.

My hat is off to your genius.
May your name stand erect
In the annals of distinction.
Genius knows no color or race.

It knows you.

I will be history

Ever since my surgery
I fear death,
The inevitability of it all,
Like night and day.
Only a flicker between here and the beyond.
The pity of it all,
No escape from reality.
Right now, I wish I am eighteen again.
Any overnight stay at the hospital
These days, gives the jitters-
It might be the last.
Should not be sorry
But, I am, for life is not only short
But also fictive
To have no enemies or excess
Is equivalent to wealth
And longevity
I envision laying prostrate
My eternal sleep.
My children sobbing my no return
I weep the pain in their hearts
Their loneliness in sorrow
Helpless, hapless, hopeless.
But time creates acceptance
Soon I become their memory.
Perhaps fatherly lectures
Or examples become their catechisms.
Will be dazed for a while
But, it will pass
They already know:
However heavy the pail of life
Can lift it anyway
With diligence and luck.

A season would come
When I will ride the streets
For the last time,
Or trail the environs
Or dine a restaurant.
Then, I will be history
After a season.
You have to appreciate.

Pain: the vilest weed that grows

This weed, vilest in the mind
If wetted by the rain of bitterness.
Yet, nobody remembers pain
But I doff my hat
For its occupation.
If physical, its throb can be choking
If psychological, a state of mind,
It can be numbing
Or unremittingly jolting
To deaden the nerves.
Some can be so biting,
They ride the hurricanes of revenge.
Without retaliation, evil
Would one day be
Extinct from the earth.

Prayer

The magic of human will
The pillar of abstract faith
Thrasher of psychological fix
Author of the healing mantras
Ally of the shattered peace
Unseen messenger of hope
Omnipotent eternal essence
Mender of the wounded trust
Tailor of shredded plans
Deliverer from the seaweeds of life
Lifter of burdened dreams
Filler of empty homes
Shaman of human miseries
Manna for nameless orphans
Miracle of uncharted seas
Doctor of the broken hearts
The dove of the hunted life
Finisher of human endeavors
Conjurer of alien hounds

Vilest weed part II

A medical oxymoron that resurrects
Those in the esophagus of death,
Or those who breathe pain terminally
In the throes of the hospice-
The halfway house to eternity.

This euphemistic weed,
An angel of mercy
Commands respectable clients:
Cancer: Glaucoma, AIDS, nausea ad infinitum.
Who says evil has no good?
San Francisco leads the Vanguard of
Enlightenment
In spite of remonstrations
From aficionados and most medical gurus.

Every revolution is born to a revolt.

Wagging the dog

In this season of inconvenience
Harsh words thrash my veins
Some tongues wag my veins
They say I am a damaged dog
Even my wife echoed my friends.
She should know better
For a while after prostate
Every nerve went on vacation
The blood refused to pump.
With blood clotting the brain
I was lucky to manage
A stroke without a stroke.
All my vitals were normal
But my stamina ebbed; my gait slowed.
In that kind of inclemency
Who wants to flip
From the mountaintop?
"You have been through much this year Tayo,"
The doctor said "Take it easy"
It's foolhardy to tumble
From humping, contrary
To the meaning of viagra- but
It worked! And it did.
First, neurologist arranged physical therapies
They were a god- send
Courage is the father of success.
I snapped from being a jelly fish flax
To being a belly of bouncing rubber,
Better to be a damaged dog and breathing, than
Being a strong stench
From six feet under.

This human mouth is made not only
For eating food but also for talking trash.

The air I breathe

In this carnival of un-wellness
I have trekked miles
Of medical mines
Snaking in, slinking out between
Prostate, balloons, Tia's
MRI's, Plavix, Coumadin and aspirins
Now, angiograms in my veins
Stent troughs in my brain.
Only the spiritual universe
Knows when and how it will end.
The guinea pig scampering
To be well, blind as a post.
To see the inside of the human heart
Is to sign a Godly relief.
Lucky to still tell the world
And canonize the festivals
Of the unknowns.
I hope no angle or devil
Slates me on their calendars.
My mission is yet undone:
My family, my writing world.
Death has no assignment
With the air I breathe –
I hope.

David Levy
Neurosurgeon extraordinaire

A person from whose head
A louse is removed
Must be grateful.
A fowl does not forget where it lays its eggs.
The man who remembers others
Remembers his redeemer—the Osagyefo.

I came to you with corrosive
Dizzy spells—a stroke gathering storm
Like a temblor garnering implosion.
You took a risk, knowing
The weather could be rough
No venture, no gain.
The stroke, forthwith eloped.
It is not only the fox,
Even the snail arrives at its destination.

Now, I have a balloon in my head
To arrest my stenosis—
The narrowing of my
Middle left cerebral artery.
At the far away specialty—
Buffalo New York Hospital
Where other wizards gathered to vet their art on
me—
The wizards who are no medical buffoons.

Without you, my noon
Could have turned an eclipse
And vegetated into a nuclear mushroom
Oh, David:
Greatness and beauty
Do not belong to the gods alone.

They are yours.
Your excellence is the mustard seed of fame.
On a windy day,
It spreads far and wide.
One cannot wait
Till the evening hours
To pay gratitude
To one's guardian spirit,
When a ripe fruit
Sees an honest man,
It drops
I thank you beyond measure
For saving my life's breath.

Cerebral angiogram

Hope is the unwillingness to die
When looking for health
In the ravens of ill-heath,
Where light seems
Incommodious to affect
The labyrinth maze of gullies
That accommodate nature's red ocean.

The doctors filled my maze
With their green ocean
Fishing for cerebral dykes
Or viscous debris that dam
The watershed of life.
My translucent corrosion
And blockage in my brain.
The thirsty fig stands patiently
Waiting for the arrival of the rain

The gods can only hear
One wish at a time—
My unwillingness to kick the bucket.
They must have heard my petitions,
Because a presence brought me to consciousness.
Still, as I awoke to life
I wondered, when the goat
Will be strong enough
To finally kill the leopard.

The sea of dry vegetation

Sometimes—
Life is like the sea
Of dry vegetation,
The genesis is an oasis of fertility—
When thoughts and dreams are foundations
Of our beings.
We feel limitless and invincible
Hardwork, success and all.
Along the way,
Life throws us a strange curve.
We wonder what's amiss.
Criticism is easy
But does not create.
Only Yarabi[4] knows tomorrow.

Often, we humans forget
The calendar fate places on our heads.

Such is this blizzard of my life.
A time there was
When I was:
      Chaka, the Zulu of my landscape
      Ogedengbe Agbogungboro—the conqueror
      Ifa, the Oracle of knowledge and profundity
      Don Quixote of social miens
      Mutesa, the King of Buganda
      The Kabakayeka of history.

We are what we think makes us
But time sobers us all.

---

[4] Yarabi– God

I hope the end is not near
I have learnt the great lessons of life
Ripe for my children to pluck.
A clay pot of water is never hot-tempered
Experience is the juice of time.

Jay Rosenberg
the Moses

Caution be your name
Adamant and emphatic
"No surgery, please. A ticking time-bomb
The brain, the engine
Of the mind,
Tinker with it,
You bait death
And dare the devil.
Who knows
What the heart thinks?
There must be another way.
Levy and I agreed,
You will be fine "
If the heart carries life
It forgets death.

When the cock crows
It never stops again.
Once it matures
It warns the world
The times of decay.

Rosenberg, the town-crier
Rosenberg, the oracle
Rosenberg, the shaman
Rosenberg, the Moses:

I like the fuss over me
Someone is present when I sleep
Levy, a frontier's man
I hear you; I love you
Rosenberg, an eagle
Whose swoops have seen

Many seasons and floods
From the sky
What better contingent
Can a dog have?
The encyclopedia,
Speaks my language,
Heaven be praised.

Now that I am well

I carry the sun within me
My nights are lit with the full moon
Every new day the dawn inspires me
I hear the birds chirping in unison with the
waterfalls
Nature's chorus of fidelity.

I spring briskly with my unseeing feet
My world fills with silence, the stillness of
happiness.
My intimacy embraces distance from worries.
My heart works the miracles of the invincible.
I feel the presence of the unseen, and the
Hallelujah of resurrection

Who has not smelt death does not know the joy of
living.
It is the warmth of the broken heart
The face does not stand the smoke
A firm tree does not bow to a storm
Ancestral spirits resist my demise
I wear the heart of the lion
A fitting tribute to my lineage.
Only dead fish swims
With the stream all the time.

My epitaph–whenever

Here sleeps the pretender:
Tayo Peter Olafioye,
Rehearsing Death.
Never rich, never poor
Always true to the core.
A Nonconformist anyway.
Tried but never was perfect.
Hoped so much
To be a scholar.
He who never tried
Is the one who failed.
A fish, he was
In many ponds of culture
In many a stream of civilization,
Some say: Colorful
But always an African at heart.

Room 304

Nigerian condition

Confessions of the moral lepers – part I

When blood rained
Darkness stifled the land
Anomie mated succubus
They brought forth their offspring: mayhem.

Nobody lives here anymore
To sniff the bonfires of decay.
When the teeth fall
The nose succumbs to all
The beasts amidst us
Scavenged dungheaps for cadavers
They had sown
To stay the reign of
The most satanic pope of Islam
The ayatollah of Christendom
The Khalif of ritual death
Called abacha of Nigeria.
He suffers a spiritual malnutrition.

Evil knows no ethnic name or race
You need only hear his arrowheads-
Sgt.Rogers, Al-mustafa,
Colonel Olu and Omenka;
His highness
Most efficient brutality
Lt. the General Bamaiyi
Vultures of ritual festivals
Confess their bestialities-
Kidnappings, mutilations, decapitations:
Severed heads, breasts and vulvas
His marabouts and necromancers ordered-
Sudanese, nigerians, Saudis, Senegalese.
Far from across the hot sands.

Surreal: hard to believe!
For one lunatic wanted to be king.
Innocent decimations
Filled his crypt...
Enemies hacked on figments-
Others in dungeons of his hell.

They cannot escape
The memory of history.
Tomorrow, their moral arbiter...
The eclipse faded
There now, the sun again
As God's true coup silenced the beast
Waiting to mate
Succubus late at night.
His satanic cardinals of doom
Now left, with the cans
And their hedonic recitations.
They forgot:
The general, a veritable evil,
Never made to walk on water.

History liberates,
Hope breathes new life
The sky, the eye of eternity
Never sleeps
It sees all things
For the helpless rabble.
Nemesis never forgets
Some redeemers always arise
When the time is ripe
In the eye of destiny, and
Ubangiji, the conscience of eternity,
Be the nightmare seemingly endless.

Moral lepers – part II

In a land infested with cancers,
When caretakers of the people,
So deadened or leaden
Assign themselves 57 mansions, a-piece,
In the land of indigence
Home vaults brimful of the people's silver,
The arrogance of invincibility;
Foreign holdings fan their dubious fantasies;
For they never thought tomorrow
Would stem their gluttony or avarice.
The country: their fiefdom
The people: their serfs,
Insensitivity: their osteo-melanoma
They lived the power-kick.

They romanced amnesia
Had hemlock's veggie for dinner
To take for granted
A people's sovereignty
Rotten to mental cripples,
Suffering Africa's mad-cow disease.
Greed, their execution in snarling volcanoes
For they lived in never-land
Bloated by their heinous enterprise.
Models of discouragement and disenchantment

Great nations nest
On the values
A great people forge.
Not moral lepers
Nor cancer-invalids
Not canards or locusts.
These will perish in infamy
And lay dumped in the cesspools
Of forgotteness.

Today is resurrection and retrieval
The people bellow their hallelujahs.
They will survive
These sepulchers of pain,
And will never forget
We pray,
These ogres of yesterday.

Do not forget

WITHIN nine days in affluence
We forget the uneasy past.
But do not forget-
Those who forget the past
Mortgage their future for a repeat.

DO NOT forget
The season, mothers dilute
Oil, water, and salt only
As stew to feed their urchins
With yam and gari[5] dough for supper.

DO NOT forget
When we baked bread
From cassava tubers for breakfast
A very poisonous necessity to survive.

DO NOT forget
When it was fashionable for our women
To line the inside of their honey pots
With roles of cocaine
Only to retrieve for sale.

DO NOT forget
When the dry winds of structural adjustment
Sparked the fire- storms of economic insufficiency
And many charred to death.

DO NOT forget
Our spring of family distrust-
Brother against brother,
Sister against sister,
Our morality went on exile.

---

[5] gari- a grit staple made from cassava

DO NOT forget
Our festivals of hired assassins.
"Madam" one professional asked
At a petrol station,
"We will help you axe your enemies,
For one hundred naira only.
Don't you have any enemies?"

MADAM, TELL US WHERE THEY LIVE
Do not forget,
How lowly we sank
In the cyclone of anomie
Many innocents were hacked to death.

DO NOT forget
How damaging and pitiful
Our inclement weather of abuse.
Nobody listened to culture, tradition or decency
Like a fish, we all rotted from the head.

DO NOT forget
How the image of Nigeria
Became fetidly skunkish
Even to our nostrils
Before our very eyes.

DO NOT forget
How we bastardized the rules of law.
We were demonized by monsters
Who grew hairs in their cavities
And mocked our ancestral beginnings.

HISTORY will carve the miscreants names in
blood.

Festivals of mayhem in the forest

Some nations forage the moon
Others visit Mars
Some work the Internet.
Others speak their Y2K's
Some amass economy
Others manage poverty.

As for us:
Busy building a nation
A very difficult task
A land of 1000 tongues
Yet dancing the midnight orgies
Offering blood at Shagamu[7]
To whiff away our pains
And wish to happen
That which we dream.
We are trying
Doing our best
After colonial ruins
It takes time.
This millennium, however embraces
Hard work not necromancy.
Human sacrifice, darkness
Of the satanic embrace
The epi- center of retrogression
We will never get far with it.
A people who defecate on their values
Give others cause
To despise them.

---

[7] Shagamu- a city in Western Nigeria, a Yoruba enclave where the inhuman sacrifice took place

The coronation of the elephant at Abuja

It was almost royal
Prince Charles was there-
The colonial reminder.
It was almost noble and heroic,
Mandela was present, the last lap
Nigeria coronates Olusegun Obansanjo –
The Generals' politician
Like many before him.
This time, was elected,
A little ray of hope
If we measure by the past.
Our lives had been full
Of obstacle illusions before.
Hope had ditched us
By many air- breaths
When we most needed it.

The bugles blared
The parades trotted
The women ululated
The horses pranced,
The air was festive.
The General draped in brocade garb;
His hat matched the national flag
Embroidered in cultural green and khaki cream.
The General now the President
Spoke in a strong voice
Principally, corruption the beast.
For which we are famously notorious.
Even the dead
Salute our brazenness;
We had no shame.

The military
Left us nothing in the coffers.
The President howled
To do something about it.
We'll wait and see;
For time is a patient witness.
This Tiger, Nigeria
Will perform a miracle
To change its spots.
He confronted the devil headlong
He was brave, the President –
Charms perform miracles
For those who are brave.
He braced up
To face the marauders
For they will put up a fight.
The world felt our fame
For we had no shame
The suffering endures.
But 100 days nigh
The president shone our hopes
Warmed our hearts and
Banned murderers of our confidence and peace
Recovered our loots.
We are on our way
Let's hope he lasts,
His team and the country.
The tree that cannot
Shed its old leaves
In the dry season
Cannot survive the period
Of drought.

The smoke that thunders

River Zambesi
In the hours of glory
Which nations frequent
As pleasure trails.
In dry times
It is the smoke that rocks.

Ironically though,
The smoke that thunders
Is the Nigerian corruption.
Festers the world
Nations resent.
We have farted so loud
On the chairs
On which we sit.
We thunder the loins
Where our stench explodes.

Let's be optimistic
That the putrescence will vanish,
If men of clean mien
Take control.
Is a new sun above
May clear the smoke
If not covered by another fog.

They start again

Two million naira
In a land 120 million poor –
Each member of parliament
To procure furniture.
All this while they lifted
Not a finger or whisper for a bill.
They start again, politicians,
Who gorge to fill
Their bowels to expand,
Despite the dry bleedings
Of ordinary Nigerians.
What affects the nose
Must also affect the eyes
That must weep for it.
The leopard never changes its stripes.
Our culture of graft
By official pronouncement.
It passes through the tusks
Of an elephant
Not the eye of a needle.
We are the elephants of Ituri Forest
Pillaging the wilds of insensitivity.
The feet of the corpse
We sowed yesterday
Showed as the mound of history.
Evil deeds are short- lived
In the memories of those
Who commit them.
We are not participants
In the festivals of the loot
Or the ceremonies of the bulge.
Hens do not attend the nuptials
Where the fox is chairperson.
Only yesterday, we failed history

We made serfs of the Mekunnus,[8]
In our sumptuous gorge
Of the national cake,
Our mind festers and stinks.
In this new share of the loot
The furniture will find
Their ways to our villages
Even the electric bulbs and toilet rolls.
The monies will be spirited
To fix our mistresses
Our Mercedes will be bigger and bigger
Our golden feet will hardly touch the dust.
No telling what we will do
In a land of 120 million poor.
If one finger touches oil
It will soil the others.
It is the mouth that coughs
That draws death to itself.

---

[8] Mekunnus- ordinary citizen

This is our millennium

The last was our calumny:
On the mountain range of racial divide.
Nothing was holy or joyous
Prosperous or revealed – at the pinnacle
But pains of black inferno
If you remember history till today.

When you are black
Or white, with a bulging nose
The Jewish slaves in Egypt and the West,
For the most part –
The African strains –
Perpetual darkness of color translates
Pernicious dungeons of perception and usage
Even God, forgot us.
The odyssey was long and arduous
Mountain steeps, every turn of history,
Oh, how tortuous to be ebonic
Yet, a most solid paint.
Among many which nature crafted

Musical of feet as inner constructs
Where humanity resides
Sepia toughness, Iroko[9] hardiness
Mahogany solidity – denied early thrusts
To avert their mis- measurement
But really, their own inhumanity –
Equal chance equal thrust.

We are all like cars-
Different colors, varied engines –
At the end, same thrusts of throttle.
We have gone

---

[9] Iroko—A hardy, bouyant, and tall tree of the equatorial forest.

From serfdom to independence
Still chained to history, economics and self-abuse.
Colonialism a chapter; freedom another
Self-abuse and greed – the indices of immaturity.

Once we were apes, Tarzan and Daktaris
At another – subhuman species, Sapiens with
tails
Rancid stinker still left over
As the skunk of past miscasts.

This should be our millenium!
We have circled the whole orbit –
Ignorance and myths –
Those who stand on the spot of yesterday
Will be left behind by today.
Each group: a merit and demerit
But are the same at the altar of humanity.
If you work for it and understand –
Slough off their scaly past,
Tissues of dead snakes.

How can a people be remembered
If the giant trees in the forest
Are soon forgotten?

The black nemesis

He who pursues an innocent chicken
Will always stumble unaware.
The thief never knows
When the farm-owner appears.
So are the murderers of:
Kudirat, Rewane and Yar' Adua.[14]
The preying mantis is never tired of waiting
Nemesis is a god of patience
It catches up with evil minters.
However long, their greed
Will betray them.

When they held power
It rode them like a wild horse
Making them to forget tomorrow.
The leech that does not let go
Dies on the dry land
They slip on the caucus of change.
Major Hamza, Sgt. Rogers, Moaamed Abach[15]
A child is what you put into him
The family mind
Is his mirror.

---

[14] Kudirat, Rewane and Yar' Adua-- Eminent Nigerians who were
assassinated by the agents of power.
[15] Those responsible for the surreptitious assassinations. The new
Obasanjo regime arrested them for their account and payback.

The presedent rides *molue* (mini-bus)

Obasanjo[10] of Nigeria

Nothing surprises like the impossible
The new millennium is another name
For strange expectations.
The president rides the mini-bus
In Africa, where the golden foot
Never touches the ground.
The VIP's usually strike a godliness
Beyond reprieve—the Sun-gods of thunder.
The wise do not use their strides
To search for thorns where they grow.
The elephant and tiger
Do not frolick on the same landscape.

In the land of the vagabonds,
Prodigals and the vain
Uneasy lies the head
That must show the way.

---

[10] Obasanjo—Nigerian President

Room 406

International scene

Mandela – the tallest tree in Africa – retires

The end of an era
In the millennium of pains.
A grateful continent waves good- bye
The tallest tree in Africa:
Most famous this century
Most heroic in history
Most courageous this millenium –
Surviving apartheid and hoisting
The flag of endurance and nobility.

Has danced the songs of delivery
      Damned the pangs of death and prided
      In the chants of Ijala[11] cantors-
      The anthem of ages and,
      The tears of forgiveness.
      Time will forever remember you.
Convinced when no one believed.
Dangled lonely when no hope breathed.
At the end, you triumphed on principle
And the world applauds.
You served uniqueness unmatched.
Now, our hearts say good- bye
Will forever remember you –
The tallest tree in Africa.

---

[11] Ijala- is the chant of traditional Yoruba hunters

Faces of infamy

Come to the land
Where time began – Africa.

Come to the asylum
Where ethnic cleansing, an anthem – Kosovo.

Come to the realm
Where NATO, a nightmare – Yugoslavia.

Come to Paradise
Where school massacres are toddlers plays –
America.

Come to the zone
Where turmoils are tornadoes – Somalia.

Come to the festivals
Where corruption assassinated old certainty –
Nigeria.

Come to the oven
Where women are doormats – Afghanistan.

Come to the Never – land
Where man, robot without a soul – Hollywood.

Come to the privileged, a town in tears
Where contentment, a killjoy – Littleton, Colorado.

Come to the home
A workshop of madness – family dysfunction.

Come to the love
A house where nobody lives – a broken marriage.

Come to the art
Where hypocrisy, a chameleon – the United
Nations.

Come to the sermon
Which harvests all seasons – the Church.

Come to the Slavs
Where life, a cosmic emptiness and lack of
meaning – Siberia.

Come to the alley
Where tornado, an Appian devastation –
Oklahoma.

Come to the park
Where helplessness is a hopelessness, – a
homelessness

Come to the path
Where hopelessness, a helplessness –
forgetfulness a death.

This island of graves

I

We all live
In this community of graves.
This past century was my witness –
My heart growls
My abdomen complains.
No millenium is as bloody
As this dying ember.
The album of history decorated
With the bloody pictures of ruin:
The first World War –
Thanks to the Austrian Kaiser
And the Serbian assassin
Of the Arch Duke –
Millions made the burnt offerings
The lust revenge and carnage.
That was the arrogance of power
And the ignorance of execution.

II

The cyclone of the second
Hit with tornadic force.
The Russians, more than any,
Lost twenty millions
As if they were peanuts.
When Hitler sneezed and scowled
Every scoundrel of the globe
Contributed their lot –
White, black, yellow or brown.
For the madness of it
And colonial conscriptions.
Of natives – the apes

That must obey.
No need to agonize 1453,
The Napoleonics of 1848's or
Garibaldi and Alexander,
Churchill, the John Bull.
In this circumference of equivalence
Were 1776, 1812, China and the Opiums.
Now, 1999 to complete the milestone and
currency.
The hundred year ones
The Spaniards too and Picasso.
Armageddon and Satanic explosions
Lived in satanic conceptions of John Milton –
Thanks for the relief.

III

Neither is the present
The best to live.
Wars of retrievals and dispossession.
Chaka, the Zulu in Africa
Biafra, Ruanda and Burundi.
The Balkans and Latin America.
Do not forget the feudalists
Or the slave drivers
The eternal blaze
Of the Middle East.

IV

One common thread:
Man's inhumanity to man,
Which speaks same tongue
And wears same colors of evil.
This Earth is the Devil's island.
Its paradisic oasis, if any are few.
I dream:
Hope lives at the feet of creation

Where my ancestors wept.
Descendants today, no better,
If only the coming millenium will smile.

V

I see the devil's deck
Playing the same cards.
No trees of prayers grow to the sky
Too angry to welcome
A desert of supplications
Or the placebos of ingratitude.
What use? Our double-edged technology
Which decimates and confuses our logic –
Children killing children,
Innocence on a permanent sabbatical.
All the meanings of modernism,
Now the issues of the twenty first and beyond:
Poverty, the stubborn leech
Greed, the sucker of conscience
With which we sleep.
Habba!
What's the meaning of life?
Tell me, if you know.
Religions, perhaps philosophies or myths
Have forever been at work.
I appreciate their sweat.

Speakers of dishonor

Those of us eyewitness
Who are no more, become the generation that
disappears.
There will spring those who read
These documents of disbelief, what we have
done.
The House Speaker of Disbelief
In the land of the Shining Seas
Hoists a flag of moral rectitude
Blab- flogging those who
Renounced his crusades – especially
The Democrats. He led a revolution,
Newt Gingrich that is, the Republicans.
His tongue walloped the president to smithereens
For groping an intern and many others.
Almost, he was a clone of McCarthy
In his torrential language of abuse
No – Holds – Barred.
The House impeached,
The Senate forgave.
A speck it remains
On the president's agendas
Not only that, the Speaker also
Engineered unethical diversion
Of appropriated finance to
His action brigades.
His party fitted him a kid's glove, but
Nemesis soon caught up.
He was disrobed for moral pollutions
Became an albatross on Republican neck
They jettisoned him
Into the dungeon of infamy
Other excesses soon followed
In roller coasters of ironical twists.
His second wife of eighteen years

Saw stench than warmth
Those who are sometimes too bright
Become victims of their own smartness.
The wife away
But, the President remains
Despite notorious missteps.

At the other stretch of the Pacific
The equatorial Guinea
Of the Giant of Africa
A deadly deception
Another Speaker of the House.
The military had ruled over thirty years
They discovered democracy
After their un-immaculate conceptions.
They returned government
To the ants of the Savannah
And the tortoise of the forest
One errant boy, Bukaiari
Who had licked the soup of corruption
With the junta professed
Ablution with the soap of hyssop--
Jostled for the speakership.
He was anointed by the new "Pressy."
Nosy reporters sniffed the Speaker's file
All his claims were sepulchers of filth.
University of Toronto
Never heard of him.
Awarded degrees
From Universities of his imagination.
His age of birth leapt backwards
Overnight, from twenty-nine to thirty-six.
He had bought the Speakership
400,000 naira from his vault--
A political and moral can of worms.
Giddy pressures mounted for his head.
Many were too happy to slot pepper
Into the president's open behind

They had hermetically sealed their own.

These two inglorious Speakers
Oracles of mistrust
Became gold- bars of rust
What epoch now lies ahead?
What heritage do they bequeath?
What models do they ensign
In the wetlands of rottenness?

The graph of intelligence quotient

In China
90% of the people
Achieve average mental development
But are manacled.
The remaining 10%
Dullards or geniuse, maniacally.
In America,
Their 10% work
The mental energy and comfort
Of the nation – inventions,
Nobel Laureates – science, technology and arts.
Their 90% and beyond, gulp what the few vent.

Credit the populace though –
Fairly uniformly progressive,
They know their rights.
Affluent in everything
Even in limitations.
Chinese, they are not
But free to think and express or spew
However silly or gullible.

America, you must agree, though imperfect –
Holds certain values
For humanity
Or certain humanity
For the conscience of the world,
On earth and the moon.
Down here, others of us
Are still dancing.
Most developing nations, including
Some pockets of Europe, still
Breathe under the guns of oligarchies
Euphemistic approbations of despots.

Peter Paul Wiplinger

You are the mustard seed
That crops the land of the heart.
You are the breeze,
That soothes the wounds of history.
You are the echo,
That jingles the chambers of conscience.
You are the mahogany,
That builds the cathedrals of truth.
You are the beacon,
That shines the past and present from the Alps.
You are the elephant,
That tramples the forests of injustice.

You are the Marshall at 60,
Still a revolutionary as if at 30.
You are the lion whose grunt or roar,
Keeps predators at bay.
You are the spirit,
That makes the most fun in life.
You are the wine,
That flows in the veins of humanity.
The tongue of your pen,
Forever liberates the home truth.

Your deed is done,
Of what use, I ask-
Is the elite or oracle,
Who does not
Contribute to his time?
You are the consummate Poet
Of Austria and the world;
The alphabets shall never forget.
The sun never sleeps,
Your name shall forever
Now stand awake.

Aujema

Top of the world in Thai tongue
But dainty damsel
Palm frond of the East.
Tall and supple a tendril,
Learning America – speak in Eng. 232
National University, San Diego
Where she is the opposite
Of the rambunctious 30
Who ironically, salivate the scholastic grind,
A rarity these days
Of the telly and the telephone.

I may never see them again:
So much kindness from their hearts.
They suffocate me with warmth
As if the king of termites.
This bunch of a class
Was jolly and mature.
Many were adolescents, managers
And mistresses of great repute.
Never late to class
Restless on grades and content,
At the ready with homeworks.
Most were international and diverse.
They are the dogs
That do not bark at parked cars.
Gregarious and scholarly dispositions –
No easy good – byes to such a bunch.

Cubism

Women are the baked cubes
In the social art of destruction
Children are the reined schizoids
In the art works of war
Young adults provide body parts
Where has gone the human heart?
On ego trips that lead no where.

The olds wither
In the bonfires of disrespect.
We have turned the world upside down
And rowed backwards in the hot winds
Of self- destruct.
If you sniff hard enough
Its stench will waft your nose.

The sun also sets in Camelot

His sun vanishes in the summer night
In the spring of his life.
The family gives fame a punch in the gut.
The fall of green leaves
Is a warning to the dry ones
Because a bad snapshot
Gives memory a frozen pain
And ulcers to expectation.
Camelot may mean a picnic of pleasure
But in Massachusetts or Hyannisport
It's the festivals of sorrow
The abundance of youthful intemperance.
An old banana leaf
Was once young and green
        never a service
        never a joy
        never a talent
        never a fame
        never a beauty
        never a hope
        never a wealth
        never a future
        never a life
So long nurtured
So soon denied.
Fate or curse
Always the devil's hand
From the incarnate to devastation
And waste.
Something must give
Look into the heart of genesis
Their ancestry must do
A sacrificial purgation
To stem the JFK's and others
Being gutted in the flames of life.
But some say they are
Soulless American icons.
Old age does not come
In one day.

Y2K

Here comes Y2K, the cash cow
The year 2000 cankerworm
A disease of the sophisticated
So much speculation
On this child:
A boy, a girl
Or a stillborn.
Nobody knows,
Everybody selling fear.
No hidden hand
Without a hidden fist.
A troubled child of the world,
Not even Christ or Mohammed.
He or she, by far
The measure of progress
Or anxiety or non-event;
Western advance and dominance
Or backwood's degeneracy.
Quite a child, so fleetfooted
Nobody can catch it;
Houdini of Technology--
Here today, there tomorrow.
It holds the world by the balls
In mortal fear:
Its irascibility or smoothness.
Students wish it wipes out
Their debts.

Miss Millennium is pregnant
Heaving to birth her Y2K.
The computer, its delivery nurse
Bill Gates & Co. :
The feeding staff.
Those who live after us
Will never guess

What we went through
Our echo of silence speaks.
The millennium was
A mystic earthquake of events
We were too charged
To be part of it.

Room 512

Cultural garden

Iwo festivals

I

Four years ago-
Counting backwards from 1999 –
Our indigenous self appointed Anglican priest,
Wanted to clean in our people
Remnant disaster or superstition
Or ancestral festival suffocating our modernity.
From time before dawn the Rebuja[10]
Traditional king,
Appoints a day in August –
Season of harvest –
To celebrate IWO – the spirit gods.

II

Sons and daughters – high, mighty and low
Afar – come home bound.
Tradition legislates, all women should hole up
All day when the procession of ancestral spirits
Roam the neighborhoods
Visiting the living; strutting and harmonizing
A peculiar cultic ululation.
It's a taboo fraught with death
For a woman to sneak or happen on the spirits.
However, they complement the festival
With feasty culinary preparations.

III

IWO festival affords the oracles
The culturally awake
To work their charms or amulets

---

[10] Rebuja—Traditional king of Osoro in Ikaleland.

Fortifications
They walk naked in processions
Carry palm fronds and satchels
White chalks, alligator peppers
Miscellany of magic props
Only real men diabolically savvy
Can brook a confrontation.
Pellets of magic pronouncements
Fly scatteredly,
Effects are not pretty.

IV

This latter day pastor, of Ilutitun[11]
A western civilized idiot
So spiritually possessed,
Was on a crusade
To mop up the heathens.
He ordered women in his diocese
Defy the cultural order
Troop out en masse
Do their chores.
To hell with the king, elders and tradition.

V

Our intellectual illiterates –
Grandpas, uncles and all –
Had news for him. So also
The academic, social and technocratic elite.
The collective view affirms
A festival is a factory of culture
A festival, a myth
A myth, a spiritual universe
A people's communal perception
Of the known, unknown and unexplainable

---

[11] Ilutitun-- a city near the poet's hometown of Igbotako, in Ikaleland
of the Yoruba people.

It knows no Jesus Christ
Whose daily life is also a spiritual festival
A myth actualizes our realities
Where is the Christmas party
The church holds every year
For the accommodation of women?
Myth is an archive of spiritual history
Any society without myth or festival is dead.
However the world degenerates
Man can never find the worm
In a cultural salt.
They taught the errant pastor to view
The landscapes of festivals, the landscape of
myth
The landscape of spiritual dimensions and
His people's need to celebrate their cultural self.
Which will not doom the empire of Jesus Christ

Say hello to:
Japan, Russia, and Italy
Mexico, England and Yugoslavia
Israel, America and the Halloweens,
To highlight a few zones of festivals.

VI

The ignorant pastor hardened
The people's resolve
Othordoxy ever since.
A people who do not have much –
Festival, on occasion
Their right of legitimacy,
And the renewal of life.
A festival is a necessity, a spiritual holiday
For a people's sense of belonging-

Oh! No!
My son becomes a girl!

From the moment my little girl
Came to this world,
My heart played a trick on me
Or, I played one of my own.
She was a boy, I believed –
Truth was a betrayal.
Nobody needs reality
More than those
Who have none to give.
For some reason
The mother dressed her
In neutral garbs all year round.
She must have learned a lesson
About to be taught me by her friend:
Who wanted a girl so bitingly,
That she fitted her third son
In female frocks, so many years.
Nobody needs a lesson
More than those
Who have none to give.

One crazy afternoon,
Reality burst my illusion.
I returned home
To find my daughter, dainty
In a female top and skirt.
Oh! Agony; Oh dizziness!
How I wished the ground
To quake its mouth open
To somersault into it, sluice a hara – kiri!
As if to say:
Truth ever changed its color.
Nobody needs reality

More than those
Who have none to give.
My sinkhole never came
But my heart.

In hind sight now,
My poor sign of wishful daze:
I thank fate that
My child is a she.
No kinder soul, a parent could wish,
A full being of family pride.
Talented is she:
Beautiful from the inside- out.
French, Spanish, and Yoruba - a polyglot.
Her ten poems in daddy's book,
Written and published at six.
Sharp as a fiddle,
Charming depths and wits.
Double promotions eternal
Awards and praise songs –
Our family ceremonies.
Languages her gift
Science and maths, her treats of relaxation.

I would rather a daughter of promise and harvests
Than a son of coco – yam head; the stony brained,
A Dundee - United or a jail – bird of many terms.
It makes no difference
If a man sees a snake,
And a woman kills it.
So long: the snake is dead.
That's my parable of life –
Many are men in female designs.

Chess of the mind

Some people, by nature, are difficult
Recondite, coy, cagey;
Nothing comes easy nor gives.
Birds in their own cage
Fenced in by instinct...
My wife: the very merchant
Of disguise and mystery.
The word "No" lives on her lips
The "yes" follows later as a treat.
She deals in the torture of silence
She means no harm
God! You need to know her
To appreciate, disingenuous bile
Wired with spontaneity.
The unimportant made so important.
At the moment of revelation
You wonder why the fuss.
The only thing to predict:
            The unpredictability
Mystery: the weapon of appreciation
She salivates – so smartingly!

Ancestors on trial

The Modernists: "Why is the present so dreary
If the past was so glorious
Inventful or eventful?"

The lawyer of today asks the law of yesterday?

Ancients: "You would not account to much
Had we never been.
We are your antique mirrors
For self-exaltations."

The Modernists: "Yes, you existed only in
yesterday
Not much to show for it."

Ancients: "Why this inquisition
The offspring of ingratitudes?
Every present, claims to be
Dandier than the era before."

The Modernists: "Well, all your praise songs,
The anthems of ages, brag
Impossible feats
We are rich in mischiefs only
Too many graves for self destructions."

Ancients: "Maybe your modern knowledge
Contuses your brain.
You're too fast for comfort."

The Modernists: "What happened to the
Many firsts you achieved?"

Ancients: "Such as?"

The Modernists: "The University of Tangore in
Tripoli,
Many surgeries without knives
The science of gaming and hunting
Why can't your children
Build on your past laurels?"

Ancients: "You forget my child,
That the chameleon has
Done its dance
It is now left for the offsprings
To do their own. We were

Not wholly pure in our season
We had our skeletons too.
            The burden of worthiness
            Or unworthiness devolves on you today."

The Modernists: "My Lord Chief Justice
 Our problem has been
            The long distance stories
Which they bequeathed us
With nothing to prove anything
We live in a cyclone
Of empty memory lanes."

Ancients: How dare you, maggots of our loins?
            How irreverent your tongue?
            What happens to cubism?
            What happens to oral traditions?
            The ancients had archives of history
            Study them.
            You have betrayed
            The ideals we left you.
            We had depth and ways to life
            Called native intelligence
            But you built a house
            Of broken fences

And a landscape of rocks
You dug gullies
Of dry rivers, and
All animals have left town.
Even the sun has closed its eyes
You have been exiled from your past
Your fibers are polluted
Your banners of glory, sullied.
You bequeath
To your posterity,
The anthills of the desert.
Their eyes sank goulish now
They eat stones for dinner
Their hearts drink the bitter waters of
insensitivity.

Now, look at yourself in the mirror.

The logic of this life

A man who kills himself
Because of one woman
Loses 200 others
That could have been his own.

Ditto:

A woman who kills herself
Because of one man, also
Loses 200 others
That could have been her own.

Only a fool returns home from town
To always flaunt his or her experience.
Wisdom is always knowing
What to omit.

If you accept:
The negative expectations of others,
You will never be able
To change the outcome

Kama Kevin King

The best 3 K's ever seen
And Fate ever united,
To teach the effervescence
Of good nature
Their youth portends.
I liked Kevin from the minute I saw him:
Ebullient and ennobled as his name affirms.
The knowingness in his eyes
Beams with confidence in his carriage.
His future writes the colors of success.
Ebbs the illogic of restraints
That ties others down.

Kama has done well –
Daughter of the sea
Her catch yields a bounteous fish
Her home firms an Iroko solidity.
Her eternal frame molds
The velvet touch of Olurombi lush
And lusciousness of the mermaid.
She did not disappoint.
Nothing but success purifies her path.

The product is already buoyant
As Exavier exudes –
Son of the gods from the deep.
No such refine ever made
That a dictionary can define,
Even the alphabets know his fame.

All the ancestry of Pat and Tony Oyeshiku
Will forever smile.

The alley cat

I fill your heart with light
Your chambers with warmth.
My deeds play notes
Of crestful laughters and songs
My love overflows with the thoughts of you.
I am a figurine in any language
Manners are a dessert
In our plate of fusion!
What the heck you jumped
Into that battle- ship?
Her breasts are huge as a reservoir,
Underskirt: yellow as a fever
Morality: the itches of an alley cat
What do you find so special?
I must be blind.
This world confuses me
Some inmost feelings
Are not worth the trouble.
Do not come back
When you feel your oats,
You ought to fail in love
As many times as you succeed.
Youth needs to lift the pails
Of oil and water – to compare.

What is it?

It is like democracy
Great when it is good
Even when bad
It is still good
A great sport without laughter

Memorial ode: Mrs. Akintoye
The princess

We felt a rage
In our bones
The furrow of tears burns our cheeks,
But the lord commands.
Celestial security
Was too late to help.
Only God says
T'was time in his eyes.

Fountains of regal flair
Sprinkled her genteel mien--
Mrs. Akintoye - my aunt,
Mother, wife, mentor,
Entrepreneur and social elite
Brewed offspring of credit
None can deny:
Olu, the dainty physician
Akin, the legal icon
Tunde, the business minder
And Dele who
Lives over the seas.

You have shown
The banner of service
The world you filled
Is forever vacant again

The lioness of regal gait
The tigress of moral rectitude,
The dove of royal peace
Eagle of towering fame
Eland of robust essence
Daughter of the traveled sea

Holy fury consummate
No fear, no justice
Your image of honor
Hangs in the parlor
of our hearts.
Adieu! We wave.
Till we meet again...

Islands of spirits in African cosmos

You Sacred Groves Where A Thousand Demon
Emperors Live:

Ojubo Yemoja and *Ogun*
Igbo Oro, Igbo Egungun, Oke Ibandon
Ubangi-Shari of the Congo
Arro-chukwu of Igbo-Dread
Ituri forest, the heart of Africa
Mahin Lagoon of the coastlines
Igbo Eledumare Fagunwa launched
Igbo Erunmole of Yoruba scene,
'Yan Bori of Hausaland
Aiyelala of Ikaleland
Idoto Shrine of Okigbo verve
Iju Valley of Idanre Shrine
Osun Osogbo supremity
Sobi of Ilorin mount.
Oke Olumo of Egbaland
Irinke-rindo Ninu Elegbeje
Kako Commander, the Bludgeon Menace
Okelangbodo of ominous dread
Palmwine drinkers, Tutuoala detailed

Pantheons here--
These spiritual entities,
Folklores describe
Are cultural atomic energies:
Creative or destructive
Blessing or a curse
Fortifications or demolitions
Myths or legends
Galaxy of celestial securities
A universe of their own

In African cosmology;
Demons or gods
Pantheons or deities
Cultural entities
Of inmost reference:
A spiritual universe of their own,
Knows no fears but inflicts their own
I salute your eminence and ferocity.

The heart of God is a poem

The ferocity of the beast is the cleverness of
creation
The innocence of babies is the language of
conception
The starry nights, or sunny days is the magic of
geography
The libido of the cock is the logic of His pleasure
The varied tongues of man is the wealth of his
diversity
The beauty of this earth is architecture of his
designs
The daintiness of women is the flowering of his
garden
The coloring of races is the richness of His art
The nature of man is the deftness of His
psychology
The creatures of this sphere spell his zoology
The passing of every soul is the impermanence in
his calendar
Everything on this earth is a poem from the heart
of God.